# IT'S STILL ME

Lillooet,
You are the Beauty
of the World,

Sayer Broughton

SAYER BROUGHTON

A Poetic Note and Credo

"It's not your poetry. It belongs to those who dwell among you. You have no creativity to share, only moments of pain and a silence where you are willing to listen to the world's view of you—one coming from the incarnate, detached view they see. You sit there, insulating the heat of pains to the beauty that is among you, always."

Sayer Broughton



ISBN 978-0-912350-00-4

A publication of:
Open Look Books

Cover photo by:
Marshall Peterson
MARSHALLTHEPHOTOGRAPHER.COM

Book design by:
Ernie Bauer
ebauerdesignstudio.com

# CONTENTS

## I



## II



## III



## IV

"Adversity is the path to truth."

Lord Byron

## Not My Poetry

I have no poetry
To share this world
My pains are misfortune,
Pathways in thought mostly
With feelings attached.
They speak to me.
Yes, I feel them,
But I think that is over
And that I am refreshed
Into something new:
A trail without spines,
But it's still me,
Unfortunately, fortunately.

## Hello There

Have you seen the silence?
The things did often go
Watch nothing; it's some-
Thing I cannot find
To open the book
Of truth. It's hard
My finger print.
I loved to thumb its
Pages, and for the friends,
It never took: a life,
My life, this book.

## Infinite Experience

This life is coming
He waited once more
For another escape
Instead of climbing
The walls of depressing
Character traits.
This is going to hurt
For awhile,
So write, I must, something
New, tell the world how
Great and wonderful,
How the powerfully present
Moment can be when
Feeling less than that—
The infinite experience.

## Creating A Singer

This life path is really
More about you than
Anybody else in your
Miraculous thunder
There, dispelling causes
For betterment
And casting those
Shadows aside.
The heart is no longer
Listening truly
For you would rather
Die than live up
To your name.

## Those Nights

I have saved
Myself through others
While calling myself
The "healer." I have
Lost many dear friends
That were already gone.
Then the moment
I spoke of their pain
Silence rang in and I knew
That I had done it:
The mystery unreeled
And over TV dinners
We shared a lifetime.

## Waking

I believe in the beauty of the day
Nighttime spoke to me in images that
Somehow made me disinterested in worldly creation
Wasn't there another world in which I could play
My spirit had grown tired as the dreams of last night
That wash through the waking hours, must uncovered
Just for a day and am I that mist who wanders through?

## Reborn On My Birthday

I am reborn on my birthday.
Every time I count my years—and
I have been here thirty-two
And counting, with the two
That are left before thirty-three.
What would come of this
Magical year of this dear
Dear boy who didn't know
But continued on, knew that
There lies possibility
That there lies new experience
That within life is a mystery
Enfolding in one's tears,
The unraveling of one's misfortunes
To see that all has been and always
Will be a perfection whether he grants it
To himself as such or more.

## Thief Of My Own Intention

Many would have taken
From you and watched you suffer
Calling you the one that
Needs help and health of consciousness.
The one applies to many you have
Crossed paths with so be it
Your curse and not theirs
They take at will and watch you
Become nothing more than
A wrinkle, so at last is your chance
To sing a final dance and allow
All the past behind you
Letting them weigh
You. All them to say
And others see the greatness
One you hid. So let go of feelings that
Ever might hurt them
Your intentions to kill them must fade
And upon this time
Now you will uncurl your brow
And allow them to be whole again.

## There Is Stillness

Understanding the richness
One follows the path
Until death does part us
Our bodies lay life
In an apple-maggot pie.
Why not justify the angle
Of lens toward the sky,
Blue with lost dream
And whispering light graces
I see that clouds do approach
Though only as means
To compare light
That does its best
To shade us and distract
From what was once there.

## Untitled #2

This prophet does not speak
In terms of ideas—replace them
With no meaning calling it yours
I like saying that you could create
That flower, to do part in seeding
And letting water flow from rain,
which is not the same. All's decided
By youthful looks upon smiling
Virgin petals she said hello to
A new friend's a mimic feeling
Brought by the wind and the breath
That would be here to free
A burgeoning word, silent in its actions,
The word that created the birth of you
Was not spoken from your
Own lips, your mouth extending
To be the creator of what
Idea or freedom from
The curse this new
Alibi brought upon them.
Delight of speaking
The creation that lays
Glance upon you young
And smiling, your girl's petals
Reflected in your eyes.
She knows this to be
For her, as she smiles
For all mystery in the world.

## Sun Flown Wind

Who are these people
And what did they do
With humanity? The cause
The just and the unrighteous
Close to their second nature.
She was close, but your
Dark appearance still
Hangs on your shoulders
Like a cap in the difficult sun-
Flown wind.

## Give It A Rest

Give it a rest.
These women have seen
You walking aimlessly
Which direction does one
Go with patents pending
For as strange scene
With apologies drifting.
I said sorry too, but
Really meant I did
That and I know why.

# II

## Changing Changed The Day

Changing changed the day.
I was the master of mistakes
It wasn't of misfortunate ways
But of unforgiving celebrations,
Of a day, one no more special
Than this yesterday's path.
The past received no fortune
For its part of the line the calendar
Re-routed every week. Without numbers it
Would not matter. With no
Day it would not all be the same
For weather and likeness and growth
Would seem to appear in green
Tones, but also in browns and
Even blacks as day grow shorter.
And even though there is repeat
To the years, she will not return
To you—if you please.

## I Loved Love's Loving Ways

I have only loved love
For long enough to know that
It does not go away when you
Feel that it is missing—
Or gone missing.
I didn't love the idea
Or the feeling as it was.
Instead, I loved the perception
Of having love, directing it
Like some drill sergeant
To somewhere outside
Of me, waiting to see
Change occur in everything
That was, everything that is,
What will eventually be.

## Treasure Waiting

Who am I
To guess of you
What comes
Forth before
Dawning moons
And elevations
Of hammering
Heart beat?
I miss you
Only because
I care
For love that
Has possibility—
I, who
Know your name.

## Following Suit

I wished upon her answers.
She'd seen me follow though
I gazed for her a-wander.
The passes we would do
And all the time
Of promise, engendered
In our ears.

We laughed and gazed
And all of me spoke.
This life is here to be.

Open the once more,
My fellow, her heart
Is yours and she is here
In sadness
For love and tears
Far less than dew

She can, she came,
She knew.

## Talk To Me Phone

What did my phone say?
Can I have your number
Imprinted on mine so
That I can see you
Locked in and dialed up
As a name to this
Slumber will soon
Forget me and I will
Redial it by heart.

## Shaded Branches

Even though there's darkness
The path lights our pathway
Shimmering glimmer shining shine
Living wanders past us
Like branches in the sun. I saw
Green reflection from her outer
Embrace, leading to the hiding
Quietude the shade
Could not and would not ever block
These laser beams of rectifying sun
Rays did praise and eyes did not shadow.

## One More Stop

The whole world cries
To you. She whispers
While screaming inside
With dimensions of left-overs,
And for new times when all
Is always great and even fate's
In on it and on our side,
So do not bear this
Calling, listen for
The next
Stop, rolling,
Not passing you by.

## Short Stops

Is this stillness
I speak of myself
As often glow
Of sparkling matter
Shouldn't I have
loved her more dearly
with my voice
and a handkerchief.
"Good day, my lady."
I have thought
of you often since
our descent from
the mountain peaks.
Wishfully, I follow
You in my mind
With heart's direction.
I have given to you
Too much of myself
and now upon your
arrival back into
my arms, I see you
In the fullness
That you are,
And feel the blessings
That be with
You forever.
"Summer Solstice"

## Walking Stick

Motions from the heart
I waited for moving
Spirits gone—still there
She asked if I could dance
To emotional turning.
"Would you be there
Still and even more over?"

We parted for nothing more
Over, until the dawn
Of new rising tears,
Rivers washed away
Walking sticks
Remember this: we sank
And dripped to water's
Edge, made by
Waking current.
My mind was torrent,
Felt the disappointment
For movement
Nearly gone.

Please me, if you can.
I'm here
As I'm always here.
There is work to be done.

## Sun Sometimes More

She wakefully opens the backdoor
Her intention was to make jam
For a friend, using a lifetime's 90
Years and counting. She had fruit-filled dreams
While Don's were of the magistrate chocolate brownies
And she, how she would find her way to the store today—
The car hadn't been working in years and
All the children had grown families of their own
Far from here, and then she was reminded
By little fairies hiding under strawberry burrs
In the caps of hidden pleasures the sunshine did dream as well.

# III

## Strawberry Patch

*"Wallace woman, 90 years old, dies in strawberry patch."*
newspaper

Picking sweetness
Time did fade
Redness ripened
Her life for years

She was no youngster
Her child-like fingers
Picked and chose,
Picked and chose.
Thirty, the count
She died with.

This day she lay
And die, the patch
She did give
Her secrets,
Layering whispers
Gone. Finding peace
In the new birth's right,
Her basket filled
With time's day  night.

## Nothing More

Be with you.
I have arrived,
Seemed so cool
This summer's noon.

I watched you
As our life grew
Bright fall
So many from the night.

I watched you as
You believed so well
And dropping
Feel the crested hill.

For one, not many
Lullabies.
No one else would cry.

You came into this mystery
Fallen star and all that's near
Bless your place
Of born embrace.

This life our life
Without disgrace.

## She's Just Passing By

She goes on signing checks
With other people's energy
Soon she will be without
The funds to interpret
Her means. I am here
As I have been here—
Wholeness my answer to
The longest lost of dreams.

I am free once more
Found by the time
Of season's breaking.
I seek no more of
This outside door,
The path is already
Upon me and should
I embrace the willow—
Its taste of shadowy
Figures to call me
And soon is the must of
Herbals gone to dust,
Through medicines of fortune's
Lust, so given as such
I now pass on the torch
To lads who are oh so
More inviting to her soul.

Good-bye, my dear
For I've lost but half the year
So see now this day
And so goes the life-long play.

## Untitled

Discuss with me
  One matter
For matters always do
  Find of me a feather
Whose flight just
  Wouldn't do.
Call on me for
Answers, my questions
Never spoken.
Live with me forever
  Because time does
  Understand.
Follow me a wandering.
My life is in a jar,
  Open. Fill me
Delightfully
And seize its passers by
Open to the wings of life
And fortunes never cried/
  Live with me in
Dreams of mist
Where steam is hot
  Not mean.

## Emptying Brook

Hey, there,
I am still
And my mind's
So full of
Empty.
My brook,
My back
It took.
I listened
Through the ages
To find us
Falling front.
I gave to them
A whisper—
Remembering the things
She often took,
The glazed eyes
And open book
And  places we sing
For certain.
I love her
And I loved so
Much, my life,
My love—
   My brook.

## Give Yourself An Open Book

Give yourself an open book
A doorway's never shut
Walk that way. You'll soon be shut
To the pains of yesterday.
Give one look and then it's gone
Forever. Though it waits in silence,
Peaceful as the break so sweet.
I came to wholeness again,
Twenty times
We walked alone
And fell onto our heads
Time and time.
We walked on home.
All we had was said.

## Let The Sea Be

Come by your side
And fill all the tides
Of grief and mistrust
Of another. Let everything
Be in the utmost the sea
Of crashing waves will want.
Now calm and not risen,
The waves stand in
Your way, for there's truth
In this day to see
And experience,
When left all alone,
You will shine to the bone,
People call, needing you
As from lighthouse nearby.
On this day approaching May
The rains wash
Your soul to the britches,
And all is sea, sea.

## Lastings

I am but one
My life is free
Bliss washed
Down this apple tree.

Falling fading
Ever present
We shadow our lives
We soon forget it.

Life became us
Yesterday
Thought of magic
All came to sway.

Follow me
O, love so dear,
I hear you beckon
In my ear.

Say to me
I come to prize
Sweetness, sureness
Love divine.

## Second Chances

Burgeoning ways
By the silence
These momentous
Times do break thee.
Come hither what may
As you stand by to say
That for all of your
Foils and fumbles,
She will enter you again.
Now, I drop down
This pen and enter a
Sleep of the waking
I'll still soon be away
And you'll always
Be true to the guide—
The light inside you.

## From Flesh To The Pen

From flesh to the pen
I have been called into May
Where searching, nearsighted, I stay.
I am close to home to home, no rapture,
No delight, and circumstances
May upon this day, say that your Time
Of changing is over,
You are a script to the heavens,
A light to the way that those
Will come enter your path,
So let go of intention, let go
Of the must for presence
Alone will not harm you.

# IV

## From Blue To Blue

You are nothing
But what you choose to do
Certain tales of excellence
Go faded by the road
Of darker times
Misunderstood pleasures
You walked on many shores
Some were there to create blues
Now shades of green open
Spring, forward the action
Into summer. Fall's reminder
Of the coolness we'd seem
To have forgotten, shifting futures
Once a cozy blanket
Now comforted by sheets of rain
Soon the sky will encompass
Our realm and blue will decide
A new refreshed sense of self.

## Garden Song

Live grasping
For rays of water
And drips of sunshine,
These plants,
My friends,
Speak openly to me
With kind words:
"We need you
Give us strength
In your showering
Gifts."

"Did you see what
We did for you today?"
Fruitful vegetable
Green-ripening strands,
I pick only when ready,
Praising the bounty
With green thumbs
  a-planting.

## For Grandma And Grandpa Conley

There is a greatness resolved
When two truths collide—
One is in marriage and the other
Is inside you when all false pretenses
Soon fade away when love
Is fortunate in its peaceful presence
Live on in through the heavens
Be the truth you all have come to be.

*With love*

## Rap Note

Do this
Grow up
Sight right
Live light

Dis Dat
Rap back
Flip flap
Time to snap.

## Sun Pants Dancing

See them as people too
They laugh while drumming
Underpants legs slapping
Each other as blue jeans
Took a pass for clinging
Thighs and undercarriages
Like freedom bells
In the whistling winds.

## Young And Curly Bottoms

Let them all be
She has curves that
Would fill your
Thoughts of things
Outside her love
Your hand her breast
Your face, the touch
Needed no more
Concentration than a child
Dipping pudding with his
Dirty little fingers.

## Angels Above

All I see
Are angels
High above our heads
Caps and gowns of loving
Light drapes to our
Spirit's hopes for us
To once in awhile
Look at this world
As perfect
Even where darkness
Shines so true.

## Spirit Smiling

Everyone you've ever known
Has everything you've known
So much, living breathing
Light and spirit they are all
Here to see you smile
And laugh in crackly tones.

## Morning Meditations

Spoon lines
Traces of mouthfuls
Exacting trails of scoopfuls
Paralleled, cross-hatched
But not without purpose,
Leavening the structure
Of the bowl like potter's
Hands, shaping a weaving
Pattern like a rice
Field on a watery slope
Terraced to perfection,
Not a waste of space
No spoonful left behind.

## Blissful Bottoms Up

Blissful bottoms up
This cup was filled with
More than dreams can speak of.
I fell in love with its warm embrace
To taste and fill this belly
A renter with a levee
To break seal of this
Desired meal.

I am now heaven sent
With blues now green
And spring forward to cling.
We guzzle the kindness the most
For now, raise me your glass
And give life its pass—
To pleasures of good folk tonight.

## A Bagful Of Rock

One was in a box
Sandy solids
Pressed and whole
By time, individually
Picked by inquisitive
Eyes, behind glasses
One-quarter-inch thick.
This one's like Easter.
Or I'll iron my shirts
With this flat
Handheld pressing,
Meshing Aztec ruins into
Tortillas. Stoneground,
Will there be a ring
Of snowy quartz
Leveled above level,
Pushed and sanded,
Winded and turned,
Exposed by a fresh
Sunshine and water-
Lacquered beach,
No longer smooth with
Pebbles, fist-size,
And palms waiting.

## Sleeping Shadows

I have come to you today
With wings of glory.
Sweetness airs the town
To morning, sleeping eyes
Do miss the light
From falling skies.
I graced the night
Sending you these gifts
Of day. We the fortunate ones
Have come this May
With seeds of plenty
And morning dew. I drop into me.
I need no shoes and because
Of this, I'm born this day
And all does feel that I am
Here and always will be—
This well so deep
Inside body and soul
I've come to creep
The shades of darkness
The times I've spent
For this good fortune
And I've gone from mountain's
Top to valley near.
My love is heightened
I have no fear
To those ones I've grown
To love this year.

## Listen

There will be a warning
Feel inside yourself deeply
He will not come for you
Until the evening
He will not be looking
For blood.
But death will soon
Awaken you both
Dear Sir.

# APPRECIATION

Dennis Held
Ernie Bauer
Marshal E. Peterson Jr.

CPSIA information can be obtained
at www.ICGtesting.com
Printed in the USA
FFOW04n1421250414
5054FF